i-SPY

nature
SPY IT! SCORE IT!

Introduction

Over the ages, the planet has evolved. At first there was no breathable air; there were no plants or animals and no blue sky. Now there is an abundance of life, weather and other natural features. Remember, you are part of nature too.

No book could include everything that you could spot, but *i-SPY Nature* includes a range of features you will find in all locations. Look under stones and up at the sky. Even your own back garden.

NEVER pick or eat any plant unless you are certain that it is good to eat, and watch out for dangerous animals that have a venomous bite or sting. Remember, NEVER go out at night unless accompanied by a responsible adult.

How to use your i-SPY book

Keep your eyes peeled for the i-SPYs in the book.

If you spy it, score it by ticking the circle or star.

Items with a star are difficult to spot so you'll have to search high and low to find them.

35 POINTS

If there is a question and you know the answer, double your points. Answers can be found at the back of the book (no cheating, please!)

Once you score 1000 points, send away for your super i-SPY certificate. Follow the instructions on page 64 to find out how.

Cumulus

These are the best known 'cotton wool' clouds which, when they are small and on their own in the sky, suggest that there is fair weather still to come.

5 POINTS

Cumulonimbus

10 POINTS

These clouds are associated with heavy rain and thunderstorms. They form at low levels, which is why they contain so much moisture, and are dark.

Above your head

Stratocumulus

These layered clouds often form as cumulus clouds spread out across the sky. They may build up in thick, dark bands and usually lead only to showers. ✓ **10** POINTS

Altocumulus

Altocumulus clouds form at high levels in the atmosphere. These clouds indicate that the high atmosphere is damp and unstable.  **10** POINTS

Nimbostratus

 **5** POINTS

Nimbostratus forms a thick blanket of cloud that usually covers the whole sky, hiding the sun or moon. It produces continuous heavy rain or snow.

Cirrus

The thin streaks of cirrus clouds are made up of ice particles; if they thicken it suggests the approach of warm air, which may lead to rain.

10 POINTS

Rainbow

Rainbows appear when rays of sunlight are bent and split by raindrops in the air. The white sunlight is split into seven colours. There is no 'pot of gold' at the end of a rainbow.

What are the seven colours of a rainbow?

15 POINTS

Double with answer

Above your head

Red sky at night

'Red sky at night, shepherds delight!' This old saying is to some extent accurate: red suggests that there is good weather to come.

15 POINTS

Snowflake

Everybody enjoys snow! It is beautiful to look at but can cause problems too. No two snowflakes are the same.

15 POINTS

Hailstones

Hailstones are balls of ice formed high in the clouds. They start at a few millimetres in diameter, but can grow to 15 cm (6 inches) and weigh 500 g. In these cases take cover!

15 POINTS

Common pipistrelle

This tiny bat roosts in cracks in buildings and trees. It feeds on small flying insects which it hunts for over woodland, farmland, and moorland.

30 POINTS

Daubenton's bat

About a quarter of the world's mammals are bats. This bat can be seen in the evening skimming over water, chasing flies.

True or False – Bats will get caught in your hair?

30 POINTS

Double with answer

Mute swan

This is a bird we all enjoy feeding at the pond, but watch out, they can get aggressive when they have a brood of cygnets (young swans).

10 POINTS

Magpie

A common member of the crow family, their nest is a large ball of twigs, often found in a roadside bush.

5 POINTS

House sparrow

Often seen dust bathing in flower beds or at the side of the road, these sparrows will eat crumbs and seeds from a bird table or feeder.

10 POINTS

Starling

In spring, if you hea a noise in your attic it's likely to be a nes of starlings. They ha been known to mim sounds from their surroundings.

10 POIN

Blue tit

Their acrobatics on bird feeders fill us with admiration. They are also the gardener's friend, as they eat lots of insect pests.

5 POINTS

Blackbird

The male blackbird has shiny black plumage and a yellow beak. His melodious song signifies that winter is over at last.

5 POINTS

Mallard

The mallard is our most
abundant wild duck
and is a familiar bird to
most people

5 POINTS

Canada geese

Introduced into Europe
more than 200 years ago
they are now native and
can be seen in large flocks
on lakes, park ponds or in
the fields cropping grass

10 POINTS

Robin

Both male and female
robins have the red breast
and are almost impossible
to tell apart. We love
them both

5 POINTS

Common hazel

Hazel has been grown for centuries, to provide firewood and as a material to build roofs. The familiar nuts are eaten by a wide variety of creatures, including us.

10 POINTS

...pple

...escended from ...e wild crab apple, ...omestic apple ...ees usually need a ...mpanion tree to ...ollinate them and ...en they can bear ...dible fruit.

10 POINTS

13

Pear

Pear trees grow up to 17 m (56 ft) in height and may have originated in China, where they have grown for at least 3000 years. Pear wood is used to make musical instruments.

 15 POINTS

Cherry

The cultivation of cherries ended in the UK during the Middle Ages but this healthy fruit was reintroduced by Henry VIII. Look for the pink flowers in May.

 10 POINTS

Sycamore

This member of the maple family can grow to 35 m (115 ft) tall. It grows seeds which are known as 'helicopters' due to the way they spin as they fall from the tree.

10 POINTS

Common yew

This strong but springy wood was the best for making longbows. In more modern times it has been found that the leaves contain an effective anti-cancer treatment, although they are poisonous if eaten.

15 POINTS

Forests, woods and hedges

English oak

The oak is viewed as a symbol of strength and longevity. Jays are responsible for planting more oak trees than humans!

10
POINTS

Common hawthorn

10 POINTS

This tree forms an impenetrable thorny hedge, which is ideal for containing animals within fields. Its bright red berries provide colour during autumn and winter.

Holly

10 POINTS

To us the red berries on the holly mean one thing: Christmas! To wildlife, they are food and can make the difference between surviving winter or not.

17

Forests, woods and hedges

Horse chestnut

In spring the tree is covered with white 'candles' and in the autumn there will be a crop of nuts you might use to play conkers.

 10 POINTS

Silver birch

The silver birch has long been associated with the start of new life, due to its outstanding ability to grow newly cleared land.

 10 POINTS

Leyland cypress

This tree is more commonly known as Leylandii and is often used in hedges. If not clipped it can reach heights of up to 30 m (98 ft).

 5 POINTS

Blackthorn

This tree is covered in 'black thorns', and blooms white blossom in warmer weather. The fruit of the blackthorn is a small plum called a sloe.

10 POINTS

Elder

Usually not much more than a bush, the elder is versatile – from the bark feeding animals to the twigs making a good fishing float.

15 POINTS

Primrose

A true harbinger of spring. What could be nicer than driving down a country lane flanked by these flowers?

10 POINTS

Common dandelion

The root of this plant has been used by herbalists to stimulate the digestive system.

5 POINTS

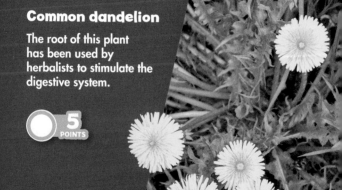

Red campion

Bumble bees bite through the base of this tall plant to reach the store of nectar. Pink flowers bloom in May and June.

15 POINTS

Common poppy

Millions of poppies appeared in the battlefields after World War I, and the red poppy has since been adopted as a symbol of remembrance.

10 POINTS

Ragwort

Steam trains supposedly helped to spread the seeds of this plant as they rushed by. Ragwort is harmful to horses, if mixed with dried grasses and hay as feed.

Common gorse

Its coconut-scented flowers are benefici to honey bees and other pollinators.

Creeping buttercup

Its creeping habit will swamp all other plants and although pretty, it's actually poisonous and gloves should be worn when weeding.

10 POINTS

Yellow iris

The roots, or rhizomes, of this waterside plant used to be crushed and the resulting juice used to make a black dye or ink.

15 POINTS

Forests, woods and hedges

Thrift

It is able to flourish on rocky sea cliffs with little fresh water or soil, while being subjected to wind and salt spray.

15 POINTS

Ivy

Ivy provides late season nectar for butterflies and a place for birds to build nests and hide from predators. It also offers food from its berries.

5 POINTS

Spear thistle

For centuries, the thistle has been the symbol of Scotland. The flowers are sought after by butterflies and bees.

10 POINTS

Dog rose

The symbol of the British monarchy is a good source of vitamin C. The bright red hips can be made into rose hip syrup.

10 POINTS

Bramble

If you brave the straggly thorns, you will enjoy the pleasures of blackberrying! And the apple and blackberry pie that follows!

5 POINTS

Forests, woods and hedges

Common duckweed

Duckweed is a strange but valuable habitat – water-borne insects shelter beneath. Up above it's the staple diet of many water birds.

10 POINTS

Ground elder

The gardener's enemy, brought here by the Roman as a herbal medicine; it does bloom pretty white flowers though.

5 POINTS

Common nettle

Apart from the obvious sting, this is a really versatile plant – it can be eaten, infused and provide relief from chest complaints.

5 POINTS

Adder

Britain's only poisonous snake is shy and will glide as quietly as possible. Seek urgent antivenom hospital treatment if you're bitten!

30 POINTS

TOP SPOT!

Grass snake

Grass snakes can grow to 1 m (3 ft) in length. They live in grassy areas near rivers, ditches and streams, and are great swimmers. They aren't venomous, but can still be scary!

25 POINTS

Stoat

You can tell the inquisitive stoat from a weasel by the black tip at the end of its tail.

20 POINTS

Weasel

A small (up to 23 cm or 9 inches excluding tail) but ferocious hunter. It eats a third of its own body weight every day.

20 POINTS

TOP SPOT!

Pine marten

Becoming more common thanks to conservationists, they have been known to live in attics, and feed at bird tables.

30 POINTS

Fern

Ferns need rich, damp soil to thrive and this is why they love the woodlan floor where they enjoy the shade.

15 POINTS

Lichen

The 17 000 species of lichens are not actually plants at all but a partnership between a fungus and algae. Some colonies may be 9000 years old

10 POINTS

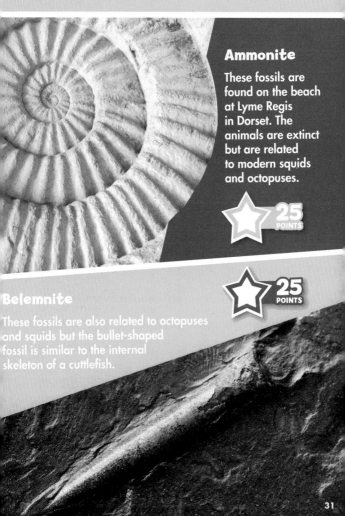

Ammonite

These fossils are found on the beach at Lyme Regis in Dorset. The animals are extinct but are related to modern squids and octopuses.

25 POINTS

25 POINTS

Belemnite

These fossils are also related to octopuses and squids but the bullet-shaped fossil is similar to the internal skeleton of a cuttlefish.

Trilobite

A trilobite is an arthropod – an animal with jointed legs like an insect or a spider. Fossils of this animal are found in rocks more than 400 million years old.

25 POINTS

Graptolite

This fossil's name means 'stone writing' because this is what scientists thought the fossils looked like. This one is at least 400 million years old.

30 POINTS

TOP SPOT

Sea urchin

Sea urchins are small, round creatures that live on the sea floor. When they die their fragile shells often get washed up to shore.

20 POINTS

Sandy beach

This kind of broad, gently sloping sandy beach occurs where the swell from the open sea rolls in, deposits some sand and pulls much of it back into the sea again.

10 POINTS

Boulder beach

When rocks are continuously washed to and fro in the water, the sharp edges are gradually worn away and they become rounded. This can take millions of years.

15 POINTS

Down by the sea

Rocky shore

Look out for rock pools where you might find crabs, shrimp, small fish or even a starfish!

10 POINTS

Cliffs

15 POINTS

The colour of the cliffs depends on the kind o rock. White cliffs are made of chalk formec from the skeletons of many billions of animals which lived millions of years ago.

Wave-cut platform

These are formed at the bas of a cliff, sometimes by the erosive action of the waves or else due to landward erosion by fresh water.

15 POINTS

Sea arch

A sea arch forms where crashing waves hollow out a cave on either side of a headland. Eventually the two caves meet and the arch is made.

30 POINTS

TOP SPOT!

Down by the sea

Sand dunes

15 POINTS

These occur on sandy beaches, where sand blows up and is trapped by marram grass. The sand builds up to create this natural land defence.

Shingle bar

20 POINTS

Double with answer

When waves approach the coast at an angle, sand and shingle are washed along the shore; this is called longshore drift.

What do we use to prevent the effects of longshore drift?

Folded rocks

Here you can clearly see how the layers of rocks have been folded, by forces within the Earth's crust.

20 POINTS

Schist

Look at this rock exposed in a sea cliff. It seems to glisten in the sunlight. It is a mineral called mica that gives this layered rock its shine.

20 POINTS

Marram grass

You will find this tough grass doing a great job by the sea – it builds sand dunes and protects our coasts from erosion.

15 POINTS

Stack

A stack is formed from an arch. After continuous erosion by the sea, the arch collapses, leaving an isolated pillar.

20 POINTS

Raised beach

The top of some beaches is made of a shingly or sandy material – this was once the beach and now the sea level has fallen in relation to the land.

25 POINTS

Worm cast

The coils of compacted mud or sand are made by worms living beneath, as they extract food from beach material.

15 POINTS

Starfish

You can find starfish as you wander along the shore. If a starfish loses one of its arms, it can simply grow another one.

20 POINTS

Bladder wrack

Bladder wrack is actually a type of algae. Wrack is a general name given to certain kinds of brown seaweed.

Do you know why it is called bladder wrack? **10 POINTS**

Double with answer

Fault

Rocks do not always fold when moved by the Earth's forces. When they break a fault is created, and the rock on either side can move.

20 POINTS

Common seal

From a distance, they look like dogs in the water and are most easily seen on the east coast.

 15 POINTS

Grey seal

They are inquisitive creatures and will swim with divers given the chance. Grey seals are much larger than the common seal.

30 POINTS

TOP SPOT!

Mountains and moorland

Firebreak

Heaths and forests can become dry in summer so there is always a risk of fire. Workers cut wide channels through vulnerable land to prevent fire spreading.

15 POINTS

U-shaped valley

These valleys were carved into a smooth U-shape by glaciers. You will also see large boulders left by the retreating ice.

15 POINTS

Mountains

Mountains are higher than hills, usually more rugged and rocky and notably higher than the land around. The higher the land, the less vegetation grows.

10 POINTS

Heathland

Heath and moorland are types of countryside where the majority of plants grow on acid soils.

15 POINTS

Mountains and moorland

Cairn

Cairns are piles of small flat stones placed on mountain paths. They help travellers stay on the right path and show them the way.

Granite

Granite is an igneous rock, formed by cooling magma. It is usually pink, grey or white in colour with visible grains.

Roche moutonnée

Pronounced 'rosh moo-tonn-ay', this is a rock which has been smoothed and rounded by a glacier passing over it.

25 POINTS

Mountain stream

When rivers are close to their source in steeply graded land, they tumble through deep, V-shaped valleys.

10 POINTS

Limestone pavement

Rainwater is slightly acidic and can open up natural exposed joints of limestone by dissolving it away.

30 POINTS

TOP SPOT!

Drystone walling

Places such as the Yorkshire Dales have walls made up of only limestone rocks. The hillsides have walls dividing them into curiously shaped fields. To make these walls is a special skill.

15 POINTS

Heather

Heather is a low-growing shrub found on heath and moorland. It is managed by controlled burning to clear the land.

10 POINTS

Cotton grass

During May and June, the seed heads of this sedge are covered in a fluffy mass of cotton which is carried on the wind.

15 POINTS

Waterfall

A waterfall forms where there is softer rock downstream from harder rock.

Which is the world's highest waterfall?

15 POINTS

Double with answer

Meander

When the land is flat, a river will flow in a series of curves called meanders. These are formed over thousands of years.

15 POINTS

Bulrush

The bulrush can easily be recognised by its female flower, which looks like a brown sausage right at the top of a 200 cm (79 inch) stalk.

15 POINTS

Common reed

Millions of starlings use it as a winter roost. During breeding season countless birds either nest in it or use its leaves and stems to construct nests.

15 POINTS

Common frog

The frog has a smooth skin that varies in colour, from green to brown. It will live anywhere that is damp and lays its eggs in ponds.

15 POINTS

Common toad

Like frogs, toads also breed in ponds. They are larger than frogs, with shorter hind legs and warty skin.

To what group of animals do frogs and toads belong?

15 POINTS

Double with answer

Smooth newt

Newts emerge from hibernation and head to fresh water to breed. Newts are carnivores (meat eaters).

20 POINTS

Otter

The otter is largely nocturnal and secretive due to past persecution. A wildlife sanctuary is the best place to see one.

30 POINTS

TOP SPOT!

Mink

Originally bred in Britain for its fur, the mink has been released by activists and is now a major predator of birds, fish and other aquatic life.

20 POINTS

Fox

Foxes are common mammals and now find their way into towns and gardens, raiding dustbins for food, especially at night.

20 POINTS

Badger

Sadly, the badger you are most likely to see is a dead one on the road. But, if you find a sett, you might be able to see one emerge from it at dusk. Stay very still and upwind of the animal.

TOP SPOT!

35 POINTS

Mole

You will be very lucky to see a live one above ground, but you can easily find evidence of them from the molehills they leave behind.

What do moles usually eat?

15 POINTS

for a molehill, Double with answer

Brown rat

An intelligent animal but a serious pest. Rats destroy millions of tonnes of food every year and can be found almost anywhere.

15 POINTS

Wood mouse

This is probably the creature that you can hear scrabbling about in the corner of a bike shed or even in your attic.

 10 POINTS

Short-tailed vole

One of Europe's most common mammals, it moves about using shallow tunnels in grasslands. Their population fluctuates in a four-year cycle.

 20 POINTS

Grey squirrel

An engaging pest – they strip the bark of young trees, eat the young and eggs of songbirds, and carry the squirrel pox virus to our native red squirrel.

10 POINTS

Red squirrel

Now a very rare find in England and Wales, you can see them fairly frequently in Scotland, but numbers are declining there too.

30 POINTS

TOP SPOT!

Muntjac

This small deer was released into the wild in 1921 and since then it has spread throughout the British Isles.

 25 POINTS

Fallow deer

If you see a deer, it is most likely to be a fallow deer. This native has been around for 400 000 years, but was almost hunted to extinction in the 14th century.

 20 POINTS

Hedgehog

You might hear snuffling in a garden at night, don't worry it's most likely a hedgehog! They have spikes for protection, and are good swimmers and climbers.

 20 POINTS

Town and country animals

Brown hare

Brown hares are bigger than rabbits and have longer ears. In spring, pairs or even groups can be seen boxing each other.

20 POINTS

Rabbit

You'll find rabbits in most of the countryside where there is plant food to eat and suitable places for them to burrow.

5 POINTS

Dragonfly

Dragonflies are identified by two pairs of transparent wings and a long body. They are normally found around lakes, ponds and streams.

10 POINTS

Damselfly

The wings of most damselflies are positioned parallel to the body when at rest. They are usually smaller and poorer fliers than dragonflies.

15 POINTS

Hoverfly

Although hoverflies resemble wasps, they do not sting. They eat huge numbers of aphids and benefit farmers and gardeners.

10 POINTS

Bugs and insects

Ladybird

Everyone likes this colourful insect. There are more than 40 species; they all have spots and some can give you a small bite if annoyed!

5 POINTS

Bumble bee

To hear the buzzing of this large, gentle but ungainly bee is to hear the sound of summer.

10 POINTS

Common wasp

The common wasp can be annoying, but is useful for the gardener as it feeds on garden pests like aphids.

5 POINTS

Stag beetle

Over 40 mm long plus the horns! Its larvae live in rotting tree stumps. In summer they emerge as adult beetles.

20 POINTS

House spider

The house spider will help you! Leave it alone in a corner of your room and it will help to keep your house free of flies and bugs all summer long.

5 POINTS

Money spider

A good luck charm since Roman times. They can travel great distances by spinning a parachute and floating in the wind.

10 POINTS

59

Sandhopper

It lives under rotting seaweed or deep in sand. When disturbed it will jump several centimetres to escape.

30 POINTS

Red admiral

This Mediterranean insect is usually first seen in May or June, though some individuals manage to survive the harsh British winter.

15 POINTS

Peacock

This large, brightly coloured insect may be seen during April and May and then again in September and October.

20 POINTS

Comma

The comma has tattered looking wings for camouflage but it is the pale comma-shaped markings on the underwings which give this butterfly its name.

15 POINTS

Emperor moth

The emperor moth is common over much of Britain. You are most likely to find one on moorland and in open country.

20 POINTS

Brown house moth

One of two common species of moth found in our homes, their caterpillars feed on crumbs and other bits of food that collect around houses.

1 POI

Large elephant hawk moth

This moth is fairly common and will visit your gardens from May onwards. The small elephant hawk moth is similar but with less pink on the wings.

25 POINTS

Answers: P5 Rainbow: Violet, indigo, blue, green, yellow, orange, red. **P8** Daubenton's bat: False. **P36** Shingle bar: Groynes. **P40** Bladder wrack: Because of the air bladders which make its fronds (leaves) float. **P48** Waterfall: Angel Falls in Venezuela 979 m (3212 ft). **P50** Toad: Amphibians. **P52** Mole: Worms.

i-SPY

How to get your i-SPY certificate and badge

Let us know when you've become a super-spotter with 1000 points and we'll send you a special certificate and badge!

Here's what to do:

- ✓ Ask a grown-up to check your score.

- ✓ Apply for your certificate at www.collins.co.uk/i-SPY (if you are under the age of 13 we'll need a parent or guardian to do this).

- ✓ We'll email you~~ ~~ and post you a brilliant badge!